MAKING LOVE FOREVERMORE

THE SACRED PATH TO
DIVINE SEXUAL ECSTASY

JOHN L

Archway Publishing books may be ordered
through booksellers or by contacting:

Archway Publishing
1663 Liberty Drive
Bloomington, IN 47403
www.archwaypublishing.com
844-669-3957

ISBN: 978-1-6657-2870-6 (sc)
ISBN: 978-1-6657-2871-3 (e)

Library of Congress Control Number: 2022915182

Print information available on the last page.

Archway Publishing rev. date: 08/24/2022

To my mother and father, who raised me
with unconditional love and taught me
how to do the same with others.

INTRODUCTION

All authors must figure out why they are compelled to write and share their stories. My roots go all the way back to my childhood. I was raised attending Catholic schools all the way from kindergarten to college. We were never taught about human sexuality. I was still a virgin when I got married at twenty-six. The only lessons we were taught were to *never* masturbate or get pregnant. The fear of those two "sins" made us feel guilty, which made it very hard to have good sex lives.

After being married for forty years and parenting five kids, I knew things had to change in my marriage—starting with me. My sex life with my wife was practically nonexistent. Maybe it would have been a whole hell of a lot better if we'd known what we were doing! When two middle-class white kids get married, they don't know what to do in the bedroom if they were raised Catholic. We were taught sex was sacred but weren't given a clue how to make it that way. I got tired of guessing, so I went back to school.

I read and studied Kinsey, Masters and Johnson, Gina Ogden, Tantra, Quodoushka, the Kama Sutra, Ananda, and Mother Mary Anna. Through my studies, I discovered a clear understanding of the differences between having sex, making love, and divine sexual union. The rewards and pitfalls of each of the three sexual methodologies became clear.

Most of what we've been taught by our religions, governments, friends and families, and porn producers has been false. (That's an understatement.) As a result, we've been denied the immense power that comes from conscious, high-level sexual union when it is practiced within a heart-to-heart union—especially when it is done on a soul-to-soul level. I personally believe we are denied this empowering information because the whole world would change from the knowledge, and those in power would lose their chokeholds on the rest of us. They can't stand the thought of losing all the money that comes with their positions.

The information in this book can be overwhelming, so I've written it in such a way that you can choose what you need in a given moment and ignore the rest if you prefer. You can always incorporate other information later on.

There is too much guilt associated with sex in our society! Tantra and Quodoushka teach us how to make sex a spiritual practice and eventually eliminate the guilt we were indoctrinated with. Guilt has to go! It was invented by others so that they could control you. *Goodbye! Sayonara!* Tantra and Quodoushka also teach us how to take the time to fully love one another.

Tantra includes a special mother's weekend, during which the matriarch is made love to by her partner for two to three hours. Have you ever experienced something like that? Trust me, when Mama's happy, everyone's happy! That joy will spread throughout your family, your neighborhood, your city, your state, and even our whole country. It will eventually surround the whole world. In time it will stop war. Happy people don't kill each other; they love each other. It's hard to imagine in our current times, but we could get there.

This is a note to my fellow elders: *Let your lights shine!* You have much that is worthy to share, even if you think your experiences have been mostly negative. Some of our greatest lessons are learned through failure, and you can help others avoid those pitfalls that tripped you up along the way.

I wrote this book to shift humanity's thinking away from hatred and suspicion and toward love and tolerance. And I can't think of a more fun way to do it for the rest of your life. So go—*do it!*

God bless each one of you.

Namaste—
John

1

REMEMBERING WHAT THE HELL HAPPENED BACK THEN

Confucius say, man who fly upside down have crack up.

I'm sitting on a bench in a Southern Cali park, thinking about my elementary school education by way of Catholic nuns. Typical. But my family life was wonderful. Unlike what I experienced at school, there was absolutely no abuse—as it should be. School was just the opposite, however—too damn much discipline and too little love.

The Catholic nuns who taught me were kind, but they knew little about life—especially when it came to sex. The word *sex* alone would get you sent straight to hell without passing go, imprisoned for life, and no chance of parole.

My scariest memories are of going to confession every Friday. The nuns lined us up to be picked off one by one. The goody-two-shoes I was, I went to confession every week, even during the summer. I'd ridden my bike a mile to church to confess my sins to Father Burro. The only sin I dreaded confessing was masturbation. My priest eventually refused to give me absolution because I would *not* quit jacking off. It scared the hell out of me, because I was sure that was where I was going. I couldn't stop though; I didn't know how to. They could tell me what not to do but not how to do it—no instructions, nada.

Guess we were just supposed to guess. The fortunate thing was that, even though I was really scared, my fear did not last. Within a couple of days, I'd know I was all right. There was always something within me that knew. Thank God for angels! We were taught so little about sex. We knew we weren't supposed to have any before we were married. And we knew that girls, specifically, were a source of temptation. They were told to strap down their breasts with ace bandages, so as not to tempt any of the boys. *Brilliant deduction!*

I believe the Great Spirit created woman's luscious, sensual bodies so that men would mate with them and have children. Furthermore, I believe our bodies were created to give each other mutual satisfaction for the rest of our lives. Are we just supposed to hold hands after childbirth? The Tantra teaches you how to be sexually active into your nineties! The Catholic Church and many fundamental churches have been abysmal failures at teaching human sexuality. Our sexuality must be expressed consensually and respectively. Suppression produces sexual abuse, as it did in Boston with Catholic priests.

After grade school, I went on to Notre Dame High School, an all-boys school in the valley. There wasn't a girl in sight.

After I graduated high school, I went to Loyola U in Los Angeles. It was also an all-boys school—double jeopardy! They were much better in all regards. They treated us well and were better instructors. These Jesuits were a great change from the Holy Cross Brothers at Notre Dame.

One of our base courses at Loyola was religion, revolving around Catholicism, of course. Catholics were the only ones who knew the truth, we were told. I majored in biology and graduated having taken courses in chemistry, physiology and anatomy. This full course in anatomy had examined, with a few exceptions, the below-the-belt regions. Did you know you don't have a pussy and a pecker? *Seriously!* We only learned the basic reproductive system: pubic hair, labia, vagina, clitoris, cervix, fallopian tubes and ovaries, the penis, testicles, and nothing else. But there was never any mention of how to make love—no way. We only referred to it as *sexual intercourse*, of course. It still amazes me that I managed to learn so much and yet so little—even after eight semesters.

My philosophy and ethics courses were also real winners, even the ethics of family life disappeared. Hell, that might have brought up sex, but no, verboten!

When my ex-wife and I divorced after forty-two years of marriage and raising five kids, I was left thinking over and over about many things. Revolutionizing my sex life was on the top of the list. Both my ex and I had been white, middle-class Catholics who knew nothing about sex when we married. We'd both been virgins in our twenties when we met, and we didn't go all the way till we got married two years later. To say our sex life had been mundane would be an understatement, so I decided to educate myself. This way, the next time I made love to a special woman, I would know what the hell I was doing. And I would fully satisfy her, knowing that a good woman would reciprocate. Then I would not have to fully focus on myself anymore. Things would flow from heart to heart.

So I studied Kinsey, Masters, and Johnson, who were focused entirely upon the physical body, with no sense of a heart connection. Masters and Johnson soon failed. All they came up with was more intimate information about physical sex. It was a lot of work with few results. You can't get good results when you look in the wrong direction. They could have gotten better results by interviewing mature women. They would have been happy to share. Sometimes academics waste a lot of time and resources on things the rest of us already know.

So along came Gina Odgen, who did just that in *The Heart and Soul of Sex* and *Women Who Love Sex*. She blew the male performance model out of the water and set it on dry land! Her books were based on her doctoral thesis. Her research clearly showed the relationship between sex and spirituality. She put the heart back into the bedroom. Women have an easier time opening their hearts, and we men should lean into that. Hells bells, it means better sex for us too! The Tantra also shows readers how to make a heart-to-heart connection and recommends to always do this before intercourse. It's actually preferable to do it before any physical contact—even kissing. That heart-to-heart union shifts your energy out of your crotch and into your heart for the entire session, dramatically increasing your pleasure. Then it's time for rock and roll.

Post sex opens your heart so that you can share real intimacy, feeling free to talk about anything and everything. You should take caution, though, and take this slowly. Neither partner wants to overburden the other with old hurts. You must instead build trust over time and pay close attention to your partner's heart. Eventually everything will have been shared, and then you will feel free to dance. It's a great time to laugh at your own follies, mishaps, and faux pas—smile, laugh, and laugh again! It is thought that the Tantra began in the Indus Valley, between India and Pakistan, two to three thousand years ago. It predates anything we rely on in modern times.

Quodoushka is the Western version of the Tantra and was practiced by the ancient Maya and Toltec for many centuries. Quodoushka shows us the nine body types of both men and women. For women, it is based upon the labia (love lips), the vagina and its depth, and the position of the clitoris (fire trigger). For men, it is the length and width of the penis and whether it points up or down. This affects the response of the woman to the doggy position and whether or not it can rub her G spot.

While Tantra and Quodoushka both show myriad sexual positions, the Kama Sutra shows sixty-four. Well, after reading that statistic I had to see how many I could think up before looking through the book. On my first try I came up with twenty-six, and the second time I got to thirty-six before giving up. And I thought I had a good imagination. See how many you can get without looking. (My favorite is the standing sixty-nine—luscious! Some Tantra sites list 488; see illustrations for just a few examples.) I wish you lots of luck!

I find it interesting that churches can't figure this out. They've been around for thousands of years. Are they illiterate? The Catholic Church taught that only the missionary position was legal and that oral sex was a no-no. I wonder what lesbians were supposed to do. Not that there's anything wrong with the missionary position; It gives you the best eye-to-eye and heart-to-heart connection. At the highest level, sexual activities are practiced in a conscious union with God, the Great Spirit, all that is, all that was, and all that ever will be. Ananda, Mother Mary Anna, and Anastasia all describe how to create a conscious heart-and-soul connection with God that is powerful. You must be actually experienced to even begin to understand it. Orgasms become intensely delicious when you can feel a direct connection with the cosmos. It is literally out of this world. When you're ready, go for it!

Ananda gives you full freedom to explore all the parts of your partner's body without guilt. Have fun! Mother Mary describes the sexual lives of Sananda, which is very new info. Their sexual union was used at its highest level, in a conscious union with God, to shift the limited consciousness here on earth. Churches have no concept of this. They never will unless they quit preaching and start teaching by example—a little "walk your talk" medicine. You know that can go down easily. Anastasia, in the Ringing Cedars of Russia, tells us how to create a space of love into which you bring children. "All children should be born in love, not lust." Enough said!

2

BENCH MATES

Confucius says: Woman who wear
jockstrap have make-believe ballroom.

When Jack Lalane was in his nineties, his wife gave an interview, and the inevitable question came up: "Do you and Jack still have sex?"

"Of course," she said. "We have sex almost every day of the week. We almost have sex on Monday. We almost have sex on Tuesday, and almost on …"

There's nothing better than a good joke to start things off. When you get far enough, you will bring laughter into the bedroom. What the hell, we all make laughable mistakes there.

One day I decided to go down to the park, sit on my favorite bench, and see who came by. It was a beautiful day, and I had nothing better to do. When I arrived, there was already a man situated where I usually sat. The following conversation transpired.

- "Hello there! You look like you need to sit down for a little rest. Come take a load off for a while," the stranger said.
- "I've just finished my book on human sexuality and do need a rest," I replied.
- "Well that's my favorite subject," he said. "I teach at the university—have been for twenty years."
- "It's my favorite too. Got me to writing my book, especially after reading Gina Ogden. Have you taught about her?" I asked.
- "No, I only teach Kinsey and Masters and Johnson," the professor said.
- "Ah yes, the authors of the male performance model. Yes, they opened up the hidden sexual practices in this country. They explored how women reach orgasm and the important role men play. Boy, we couldn't do without them!" I enthused. "I also do counseling on the side. Well, here comes someone else. He's very interesting, eh, professor?"
- "Sure is," he replied as he scooted over to make more room on the bench for the newcomer. "That's Confucius. He was in one of my classes."
- "Confucius," I said, extending my hand for a shake. "I'm Troy Menage, and this is Professor Stiles. Remember him?"

- "I surely do," Confucius said. "Some of our discussions got a little crazy. Did I hear you say you're a counselor now?"
- "Yes! There are many times when I feel like I need counseling," the professor interjected. "Confucius, much of what you do is superficial and not that fulfilling."
- "Yes, there are times I feel that way," Confucius said.
- "As a sexuality professor, I see that."
- "That may be, but pornography is based upon the male performance model you gentlemen are so proud of," I said.
- "True enough, true enough," the professor conceded. "There must be a better way."
- "But I do my best to keep your profession out of trouble—like one of your porn friends. She came in here with her heart broken, sobbing because she thought her boyfriend was unfaithful," I said. "It's no surprise in your business where you are geared to love and gun. She'd been there once before, upset and crying. I calmed her down with quiet music, and I advised her to slow down. She said she couldn't—too much money and too much fun. What do you think, Confucius?"
- "She should just keep from crying," Confucius replied. "It's part of the business. Fuck and run gets to you after a while—too much here today and gone tomorrow. Sometimes I want to quit too, but I don't know how. It's all I've ever done, and it's fun. Though the older I get ..." His voice trailed off. "Professor, what would you do?"
- "First thing is to get away for a while and honestly look at yourself. Find out what you are good at and really

like to do," the professor replied. "By the way, how old are you?"

- "Fifty-one," Confucius replied.

- "That's kind of old for your business," I said.

- "Yes, it is. Most retire at forty-five or fifty when looks fail and bodies sag. And it can get old when you've fucked everyone on the planet and just don't feel fulfilled like you used to," Confucius said.

- "You know, you really need to get away and do some deep thinking. You might think about starting a dating service for folks in their forties and fifties—especially the ones who have been down the road and are burnt out. After all, with your long history of sexual encounters, you know most of the traps folks want to avoid. They still want a lot of sex but want to avoid all the pricks and thorns they've encountered over the years," the professor said.

- "I know all the traps and how to avoid them," Confucius replied. "But I don't know how to run a business. I need a savvy woman who's been around."

- "You said a savvy woman? One who's *been there*? Stella Law may be the one," I said. "She's been through four divorces from four unfaithful husbands. She still enjoys sex but is afraid to date. Stella was a top corporate secretary, and whenever I need something done I call her. She's amazing! All I have to do is outline the problem and she gets it done—and well! Give me your phone number. I'll have her call you. Just one thing—I think you're sincere, but if not, I will call it all off. Understand?"

- "Yes, she sounds just like the one I need," Confucius said with a smile.
- "Father, come sit down for a while. Let me introduce you to Professor Stiles."
- "Good to meet you. I'm Father Burro."
- "Good to meet you."
- "Troy tells me you taught human sexuality at the university for years."
- "Yes, specializing in the subtleties revealed by Kinsey and Masters and Johnson."
- "Did you study any other research?"
- "Only a little of Gina Ogden's work. She said women play a very important role in the bedroom—even as equal partners! Makes no sense to me. Me, I've always led in the bedroom. Nothing else can work as well. We are the driving force!"
- "What do you think, Father? You've had a lot of people confess their sexual sins to you."
- "Well, that is the way it seems to most men—even me. But I've listened to young girls cry because they were treated as mere sex objects—even when it felt good to be used. One pussy was as good as another. There was no heart in it. These girl need a heart connection. Otherwise they feel empty. What about your wife?"
- "Well, sometimes, but she gets over it."
- "Professor, I doubt it. I really think you would like the best for your wife. Get Gina Ogden's book and read it—*together*. You will be amazed by how your perspective changes. And by how much your sex life improves."

3

WOMEN'S PERSPECTIVE

*Confucius say: Panties not best
thing on earth, but next to it.*

- "Women are more sensitive than men by a long shot when we are treated right—especially in the bedroom. We reciprocate. Yes, we do. That is our innate nature. I've been sitting next to you on the other bench with my friends, and we've heard a lot of confused opinions. We'd like to talk to you men and express our insights. My name is Mary Smith—yes, the original one. I have two boys and three girls. Most are prepubescent. It's the older boys I'm worried about, Father Burro. They masturbate all the time and can't seem to stop.
- "I wish they would do it less often. They really are good boys. I'd just like to not to change their sheets so often.

I know the Catholic Church forbids that, but why? It's not harmful, and they don't hurt anyone. It gives them a safe way to handle their sexual energy. And they do enjoy it. I want my kids to be happy! Is there a biblical basis for this teaching?"

- "I don't know. I think it is based upon a *papa encyclical*."
- "So are you saying that when the Pope speaks it becomes law?"
- "Yes, I am."
- "Then that means he has the authority to invent new laws and the Bible be damned?"
- "No, but—"
- "I've heard protestant ministers preach the same nonsense, but you priests have a *pope* to back you up with an 'official encyclical.' You're slick! As slick as you are, you forgot one thing. What are the boys to do with all that God-given energy? Typical Catholic BS, telling you what to do without any alternative. What the hell are they supposed to do?"
- "Well, Mary, I have been in the porn business for thirty years. All boys jack off—perfectly natural. You're right—what the hell are they supposed to do with all that crazy energy? Even priests jack off—including you, Father Burro. Do you feel guilty? Those boys come to us wondering what to do. Most of them want the real thing, a hot mama."
- "Troy, we haven't heard much from you!"
- "Well, Confucius, I agree with those who know it's natural. If it isn't, we're all going to hell, and there will be plenty of priests and nuns for company. Maybe then

they can teach us something. By the way, there's no biblical scripture that forbids masturbation. Two verses are usually cited, but the meaning is only implied, giving churches license to interpret it any way they want. Read it yourself, and make up your own mind."

- "If you wish to control that energy, you can using the Tibetan Rites, #6. You will have to get an old edition. The new editions dropped #6 and only go to #5."

- "Same story I encountered in my youth when I was told to stop. The priest couldn't tell me how to quit. I've since learned that when someone in authority tells me what to do without telling me how, they either don't know or don't care. If you can't show me how you do it, you're full of it."

- "Well, Mary, being your next door neighbor, I'm also concerned with your boys' behavior—especially when they start to date."

- "JoAnn, me too."

- "Having three girls too, you're going to have your hands full. I know I already have one of my girls masturbating too. The other two seem to be OK. It's really humorous. I used a vibrator for years. I have a much higher sex drive than my husband. He does his best, but it isn't always enough. We were able to sit down and talk about it, and he said it was fine. He knew I appreciated what he tried to do. He said to use it whenever I wanted because he loved me and wanted me to be happy."

- "JoAnn, you have a good one!"

- "So with his blessing I sat down with my girls and taught them how to use a vibrator. Told them they could masturbate or use a vibrator. Gave my oldest girl a vibrator for her thirteenth birthday. She just grinned and said thank you. Her younger sisters teased her about her super-cool machine. Wanted to know if she could go to the moon in it and if they could come too."

- "Masturbation isn't my main concern. It's dating. You can handle masturbating much easier than dating. So, rather than preaching at my girls, I've given them a few simple hints. First of all, dating is preparation for marriage. So how do you pick a good mate? Any number of boys are going to ask you to have sex with them. How do you choose? Ask yourself if he is someone you would want to raise children with. When he asks you to have sex, is he looking in your eyes or down your blouse?"

- "Well, a friend of mine tells his granddaughters that when a boy asks, they should say, 'OK, what's next?' Baffles most boys. But the bottom line is, do you love him?"

- "Well, Troy, that's fine, but my old professor really stressed safety—especially in these days when STDs are so common. 'Use condoms,' he would say. 'Two or three,' he would say, half-joking. Some churches have big problems, but they're more concerned with scriptures than the safety of their kids."

4

DIVORCE AND RELATIONSHIPS

*Confucius say: Woman who suck
dick come long, long way!*

- "Father Burro, you must face a lot of problems from parents."
- "We do, but all our advice seems to do little good. We can't stop divorce, even with our parental guidance courses. Current divorce rates average 10 percent in the US. They vary from state to state, with Arkansas at about 26 percent, the highest, and New York at 5 percent. It doesn't please us, and neither does the high infidelity rate of 15 percent for women and 25 percent for men. We aren't reaching them in church or in academia, and counselors like myself aren't reaching them either. Excuses, excuses! Our marriages lack the

strong love that's necessary for longevity. People just don't feel closely connected."

- "Maybe that's why porn is so popular today. When they feel unloved and unimportant, they come to us. We love that, but it doesn't solve the problem. We don't see pornography as a problem. It's one thing they can rely on. We do love what we do, but too much is too much."

- "Well, as priests we see it as a major problem. Sometimes it seems all our advice does little good. Do any of you women have a solution?"

- "Maybe. I'm speaking for a friend of mine who gave her son a copy of *Playboy* when he was a teen and told him to read it. She did let him know that most women he'd meet would look just like her and his auntie— not beautiful with big, gorgeous boobs. Enjoy it. But remember when you meet a woman you love you won't care much about her looks or whether she has Cs or Ds. That can be a real measure for your love. Is it centered on her face or on her breasts? Maybe that's why they say love is blind."

- "Well, JoAnn, what do you think?"

- "Sounds like a good idea to me. Trying to suppress sexuality is a waste of time and just leads to abuse. Check the Catholic Church's Boston massacre. Only honest communication helps. I always look directly into the eyes of my children and do the same with my loving husband."

- "Counselor, what is your experience?"

- "In time, we get very close to our clients if we give them the time to open up. Trauma doesn't just walk away.

Kind, patient listening will open even the most closed heart. Then they can feel free to talk about anything, sexual abuse, infidelity, and even their secret fears. When they open up all the way, nothing is impossible. Infidelity comes up then. Usually there's a lack of commitment from one or both partners—also a real lack of understanding. You can't commit to something you don't understand. My job is to get them to sit down and treat each other as equals. There shouldn't be any competition in the bedroom. It's a team effort, and no one is the quarterback."

- "Father Burro, what do you usually encounter?"
- "The biggest one is a lack of commitment—usually due to just marrying too young. I can't stress strongly enough that marriage is long-term, especially if you plan to raise children. Divorce really upsets the whole family, especially young and sensitive children who get caught in the middle of it. Sometimes it breaks my heart, and I feel helpless. Marriage classes do help. But ..." His voice trailed off.
- "All right, what about domestic abuse? It's even common in unmarried couples."
- "There's one church that has a very forward-thinking program. They have a large congregation with lots of singles who aren't getting married—even they experience a lot of abuse. Their church has this incredible offer: Attend our marriage course and our domestic abuse course, and we'll marry you in our church and pay all the expenses. It's a full one-year program. Now that's real

Christianity—taking care of your brothers and sisters. I don't know about you, but that's a deal I can't refuse!" "Thanks, Troy. They do put their money where their mouth is. Although domestic abuse is serious, it isn't the top reason for divorce. According to womensdivorce. com, it causes 10 percent of separations. Infidelity causes 27 percent; 18 percent say they've grown apart; 17 percent fail due to incompatibility; 8 percent because of money; 1 percent because of children; and 21 percent responded 'other.' When I counsel couples, I encounter all these causes. Wrong religion, wrong race, wrong politics, and on and on. I advise them to talk out these differences before marriage. After marriage it's almost impossible. If they can't do it with their friends and relatives, they should seek counseling with a priest or any good counselor. We always tell them there will be differences between them. They are on a new journey, a long, tenuous expedition. The bottom line is, do you love each other enough to work out the differences? If not, that's OK. Find someone you're really compatible with. You've already 'failed' once, so take your time. Don't just rely on heat to drive the equation."

5

PRIDE IN YOUR BODY

*Confucius say: Man who fight with
wife all day, get no piece at night.*

If you don't like your body, you can reasonably change it through good nutrition and exercise. You do not have to drive your body. Take the time to tune into it, and it will guide you. The good Lord gave us incredible machines— with instructions. It's a given that some women are born with luscious bodies and some men as studs. The rest of us fall somewhere in the middle. Children don't have any control over their genetics or their parents' lifestyles—or much else. Take what you have and make the best of it. Ray Charles and Jose Feliciano were born blind, and look where they went! Many who were born with a lot more sit on their butts and watch them go to the moon. We can all go to the moon. It just requires a smile on your happy face.

Here's an exercise I think is very helpful. As a male, it gives me an appreciation for the female body (not what I learned in catechism class). According to the Bible and Edgar Cayce (worth checking out), God created Adam, then Eve as a helpmate. When you compare the two, it looks like God got a lot better as He went back to the drawing table. (Hire that guy!)

Adam's face: plain	Eve's face: pretty
" lips: small	" lips: full and sensuous
" torso: plain	" torso: beautiful, luscious
" hips: flat	" hips: full and curvy
" legs: plain	" legs: taper sensuously

Looks like God created as Volkswagen and then a Maserati. I know which one I want to drive. How about you? No matter which one you have, you can give it a new paintjob, new headlights, and sexy new taillights. Drive on, baby! The road is yours.

6

EXERCISE AND NUTRITION

Confucius Say: Learn to
masturbate, come in handy.

Exercise is a dirty word. You don't need to exercise, but your body needs movement to be healthy. You don't have to go to the gym five days a week and drop twenty bucks to drop twenty pounds. Some of the best ways to shed weight are dancing and swimming. Both are a lot of fun and don't require a gym membership.

If you like sports, you can't beat basketball. Walking is great exercise and requires no special equipment. The bottom line is do what turns you on; it's the only thing you'll stick with. Yoga and tai chi have a long history behind them and stay popular, even as other exercise fads come and go. They don't overload your system and are very good for long-term health, including that which hangs below your belt. I know a woman who is seventy-seven and is just now having the best sex of her life. She has practiced and taught yoga for over twenty years and has a younger lover who is about seventy. He treats her with respect and never asks her for anything. She's the happiest she's ever been in the bedroom.

Women can do Kegel exercises, which continue to give better health and orgasms. If men stay in shape, they'll perform better in the bedroom. You don't have to bust your butt either. "No pain, no gain" is a bunch of macho BS. Three days a week can give you significant gains. When I was in high school I started lifting weights. The year before, I'd started working in construction. It kicked my butt—barely survived, but I had to go back the next year since it paid my tuition for college. The nine months of my junior year did the trick. I went from 120 to 150 pounds during the school year. The next summer was not a cakewalk, but I wasn't begging for mercy. I never pushed to the pain limit, as it made no sense to me to do so. Hell, I don't like pain. But as they say, to each their own poison. All this was done without a coach, but having a mentor can be a great help. I just worked out in the garage rent free, but if you're really serious or after a spot on a team or want to go to the Olympics, go for it.

I can't overstress the need to pace yourself. Overloading your body usually leads to injury and pain, and you'll probably lose a lot more than you gain. Balance is one big key to a healthy lifestyle. We don't have to compete with everyone!

7

NUTRITION

Confucius Say: Man who eats pussy does sweet lip service (one serving only. Sorry, none on Sundays).

The story of the three little pigs illustrates our major diet choices. The first pig builds her house out of straw, and the first strong wind blows it away—no strength. *Sayonara!* That's just like eating junk food. Sure, it looks good—but! The second pig builds her house of sticks. It holds up well until a heavy thunderstorm levels it. That's like eating supermarket food. The third pig builds her house out of bricks, and it lasts a lifetime. Straw food will lead to a very early death. Stick food will lead to an average lifespan and some time for dancing. Brick food gives you a full lifetime with enough energy for a lot of dancing. Much of this is based upon my personal experiences, and I'm a master organic gardener and look and move like I did twenty years ago. Sometimes it's not easy, but it's been worth it.

There are too many crazy and confusing diets out there. Oops, wait a second—here comes another one. So what do you do—just take chances? One of the very best options is the Mediterranean diet (please see illustration). It's been around since 1970 or thereabouts and has been the one I have followed for the last forty years. I get around very well. I go fishing and hiking with relative ease. What slows me down is glaucoma. My eyes are weak. I have worn glasses since sixth grade. It seems as if we all have at least one or two physical weaknesses. My lower back is my other issue. Special breathing techniques have solved that problem, and I still garden. My lower back gives me fewer problems at eighty than I had at sixty. It does work! Gardening gets you out into the sunshine and fresh air, which are two of the greatest gifts we have been given by the Great Spirit.

There are several other Mediterranean diets. You can choose from ones that are lighter on grains and heavier on fish or with a light meat. Vitamins and minerals are a must. Our food supplies are contaminated and depleted—even some organic farms. Community support is also a must for emotional balance, better health, and more laughs. Your longevity is increased. You will see some results if you work with someone who has common goals. Good nutrition takes commitment, but go easy on yourself. Don't shoot for the moon, or you may end up shooting yourself in the foot or elsewhere. Change only one or two things at a time each week or month. This way you will not feel guilty by setting your goals too high. This way you will keep moving. You don't want to die on the vine; that can be sort of painful.

Here are some food combinations I have found helpful: (1) Whole grains and pasta are very good with fish and seafood. (2) Dried fruits and nuts are especially good for breakfast. Nuts are one of the highest vibrational foods. (3) Red wine with spaghetti sauce balances the acidity in the tomato sauce, and (4) lime beer does the same for Mexican dishes that have red salsas.

Always seek balance that is emphatically your own in your diet. Like I did, you will have friends and others make suggestions. Most will be in good faith, but do they really know what you need? Do you know? I went through years of this to no avail. I just became an expert in confusion. Some of the best advice I've heard is to always have a raw portion of your meal. This gives you all the raw elements that are often lost in cooking like vitamins, minerals, and antioxidants.

Long story short: I went to a chiropractor, and we did some advanced testing using his kinesiology techniques. I went in with a complete list of the foods I mainly ate. Beef tested *no*, and so did pork. Chicken was OK. We did the same with a list of dairy products from milk and kiefer. Yogurt and kiefer were fine, but milk was questionable. We even checked oils: olive, corn, sunflower, safflower, and canola. All were checked as good except for canola. Canola oil is produced in Canada, which is where the name came from. It's produced from rapeseed. Wonder why they changed the name? Rapeseed oil is toxic. Olive oil is at the top of the list. I use a lot myself. All oils should be in their natural state, except 30W. All oils should be cold pressed. Chemically extracted oils contain some toxic residue.

You can go to any competent chiropractor or naturopath to do this testing. For fifty to a hundred bucks, you can cut out most of the confusion. You should call ahead of time, as not all practitioners do this testing. While you're at it, don't forget to check prices. I have often found that some very confusing problems have simple solutions. If you talk to your angels, ask them first.

Talking to my angels solved my problem with my chickens. They laid great until November, then nothing till March or April. That was normal; chickens quit laying in the winter due to short daylight hours. So I asked my angels what to do. They said, "Send them love!" OK. But how do I send love to a bunch of dumb chickens? Not really knowing what to do, I just sent them my gratitude for all their eggs. Just sent my appreciation while I tossed out their feed on the ground. I never said a word, I just did it telepathically. I couldn't bring myself to do anything more to a bunch of dumb chickens.

It turned out chickens aren't so dumb. We treat our bodies like garbage cans. We tend to dump anything in them, but chickens don't. Some things they don't touch. They won't eat tent caterpillars but will devour tomato hornworms. Dropping a tomato hornworm in their pen creates a real circus. The chicken that grabs it takes off, and the race is on. All the others try to grab it, and finally one does. She races to a corner where she can pin it down in safety, drops it on the ground, and starts pecking it to death. But then another grabs it and runs, and another, and so on until one is finally able to devour it in a safe place along the fence line. I loved watching this merry-go-round and did everything except place bets. My bookie was out of town.

For those who don't raise chickens, Vital Farms produces the best commercial eggs I can buy. There are also small local farms that produce high-quality organic eggs. Your local health food store will know. It's always best to raise your own organic food when you can, but when you can't, support those who do. We can't afford to lose the best we have. Who will we have left when they are gone? You can always join a food co-op. There are very interesting people who are fun to be with.

8

HUMAN SEXUALITY

Confucius Say: Man who suck
nipples fly to milky way!

After reading all the sources I could, it became apparent that
they needed to be summarized in a logical manner. There
were too many competing opinions where the authors were
stuck in their own worlds. Kinsey and Masters and Johnson
thought that the only solution was the performance model
they taught. (Sorry, they did not supply any models.) Gina
Ogden was far more open-minded and showed the female
perspective. It makes me wonder why the men forgot about
women. Ogden recorded one woman who could orgasm at
the sight of a beautiful sunset. Why not? Women now know
how to have a nipple orgasm. Some like mouth orgasms. It
sure beats any food I ever ate or cooked. She describes many

other incredible experiences that women have. Along with Kinsey and Masters and Johnson, Gina Ogden is the other academic source covered in this book.

Tantric sex focuses on the release of your kundalini energy that lies at the base of your spine. I read *Tantric Sex for Men* by Kerry Riley and Diane Riley, who are the co-creators of *The Secrets of Sacred Sex* video. They show how to raise the energy out of your root chakra up to your heart chakra. It will shift you out of your crotch and into your heart. When you are heart-centered, magic happens. You become as one in body and mind as mutual respect and honor resonate throughout the bedroom. Eventually it resonates throughout your entire family! Tantra uses many methods to raise this energy up to the heart chakra and even higher. You can go all the way to the crown chakra, where you will experience levels of pleasure unheard of (except in your bedroom).

One sweet method has the couple lie on their sides with both legs spread apart, and their sex organs are in contact with each other for five to ten minutes. It's useful when there just isn't enough time but you want a sensual way of saying I love you with a promise of sex later. This position can be used any time you need to be nurtured—when you really know you're out of sorts and need someone very close to you to say they care. This can be done at any time, but there is an agreement that when you ask for this pleasure, your partner has five to ten minutes to act. When I get into something, I find it hard to break away right away. My ex was just the opposite. She could just drop anything. It gives flexibility without pressure to perform. I like this!

Another method I like is very intimate. The man sits on a pillow with his knees bent underneath. He has a full erection. When his partner is ready, she mounts him. He can't move until she does, so it gives the woman full control of depth and penetration. Tantra has sixty-plus positions, and you can have a lot fun with them.

Quoudoushka, the teachings of the Nagual, is the Western version of Tantra. It was practiced by the ancient Mayans and Toltecs. One of the most interesting things they teach is the physical difference between men and women. There are nine different types of sexual anatomies for both genders. For men, the types are based on the shape, length, and thickness of the penis. Length goes from about four to eight inches. According to some men, it goes to infinity! For women the types are based on their labia (love lips), mainly on the different shapes and difference depths of their caves. It's also upon the position and depth of their fire trigger (clitoris).

As with Tantra, Quoudoushka emphasis maximizing orgasms and taking the time to do it properly—your choice, not your church's. You can now buy a book that teaches this: *Leading the Orgasmic Life*. Don't look for this in your church library. Unlike what the Catholic church teaches we were created to be happy, not to run around in "sackcloth and ashes." We were created to be happy. Love and loving kind of fit the bill. If you read Quodoushka, read the forward by Thunder Strikes. He expresses what I have tried to say far better than I have.

I know I have hammered churches because they minimize the legitimate pleasures of sexual union and often associate it with guilt. You know, at some level they know what they are doing. I think most of us would rather stay home and skip guilty churches and make love and experience high-level orgasms. I've never experienced bliss like an orgasm in church. After all, it was God who created our wonderful bodies that can experience extreme pleasure. So if it is preached otherwise, those "teachers" need to talk to the man upstairs and tell him he screwed up.

The Kama Sutra is a mind blower to a Catholic boy who thought there was only one legal sexual position—the sacred missionary. There are actually seven main positions: missionary, cunnilingus, blow job, sixty-nine, cowgirl, anal, and doggie. There are twenty-two sex positions: sixty-nine, anal, blow job, cowgirl, crisscross, cunnilingus, doggy style, face to face, from behind, kneeling, lying down, man on top, oral, rear, entry, reverse, right angle, sideways, sitting, spooning, standing, and woman on top. There are at least currently 428 variations and counting of these (different sources give different numbers). That ought to keep us busy for a while. Check with your lower back first. All these wild positions give the Kama Sutra a distorted reputation in the West. In the East they see it as a way of exploring and expanding intimacy to live a full spiritual life. Free the body, free the soul. As above, so below. Any way you look at it, it makes life a lot more fun. What a way to explore your spirit. Sign me up!

The only position that causes a lot of controversy is anal, especially among the Christian community. There's much confusion—which is normal in that community. It couldn't be otherwise since there are over 120 different Christian religions in the US alone. Nonetheless, in the account of Sodom and Gomorrah, the gay men in town try to rape two angels, who are posing as men. It is assumed it was anal, though there's no reference that specifies. It could have also been oral.

Ananda's book is called *Making Love to God: The Path to Divine Sexual Union*. You won't find this book in your church's library, either. It focuses upon healing your sexual misconceptions and the guilt associated with them.

Chapters include:

I.   How we came to misunderstand our sexual energy. The basic problem, misinformed minds.
II. Transformed View of Sex and Sexual Energy. Faith and Sex.
III. Blocks to Transformation. Fear and Guilt.
IV. Following the path to Transformation
IV. Using Divine Sex Energy. When practiced, ecstasy is the norm.

I know few of you are ready for this, but I wanted you to know your full potential. It will probably be in another lifetime.

Anastasia describes in the *Ringing Cedars of Russia* how to use divine sexual union to raise a perfect child. God and the benevolent forces of nature are in perfect spiritual union. They refrain from sex for one to two months. During that time they meditate and focus on the perfect child they want. The results are mind-blowing. She also says the union is so intensely balanced that the memory could last you a lifetime. You wouldn't even want any more sex. This fulfills one of her major principles—that all children should be born in love, not lust. I wish I would have known that when I was young.

9

GUILT TRIPS

Confucius Say: Foolish man gets wife grand piano. Wise man gets upright organ.

All of us carry guilt—often because we've been misjudged by others. Some of these guilt trips are mine, and some are from my friends. Many of us have been in court and watched a judge unfairly accuse a defendant of a crime. It's obvious to us but not to him or her. Most judges are no smarter than you and I. They only think they are. When a judge cannot be fair, he or she is only judging themselves. If they can't be fair, it's because they feel guilty and cannot forgive themselves. They can't give you what they don't have: compassion for themselves.

Amara Charles, author of Quoushka tells a cute story. When she was in high school, she and a girlfriend decided to go on a double date with a couple of boys "to have some fun." Later that week she was telling a friend about her date and how excited she got when he pulled her pants down. Her friend said, "He did *what*?" That taught her to be careful of who she talked to—made me laugh! I've been there and done that.

This is a good example of how others judge you without even thinking, especially when it's based on a church's teachings. That girl was more in love with her church than her own friends. Good friends are hard to find. This is a good example of how others judge you as guilty. Amara was smart enough not to take on her friend's guilt. Guilt does not only come from yourself—there are others who are more than willing to help out. A word of caution though: there are many people who have good intentions but lack the wisdom to understand them. Common sense is hard to find.

I can't overstress how important it is to take care of our kids—I have five—the best we can, but I also realize how unfair our economic system is. It leaves many poor people suckin' eggs, and wishin' they had some to eat! Most parents do the best they can under the circumstances. We have been seduced into thinking we are only worth a minimum wage, not a living wage. Where in the hell do corporate CEOs get the notion our kids are not as worthy as theirs? Maybe it is in hell. If anyone needs to feel guilty, it is them. They don't have the balls to even try to live on a minimum wage. If anyone needs to feel guilty, it is them. They are experts at transferring their guilt to the guiltless.

If any group gets a major guilt trip laid on them, it is the gay community. It's mainly due to their so-called "sinful behavior," mainly sodomy. Sodomy is a slick biblical term for anal and oral sex. Anal sex is practiced by the entire world. You can get on any porn site to see straight couples enjoying the practice. Try the Russian sites—they're nuts. Both Tantra and Quoudoushka approve it. I personally disagree, but that's mainly for health reasons.

John Brown University here in Arkansas ran a study on pornography. They found that 50–60 percent of Christians were addicted to internet porn sites. Nothing has changed in Arkansas or the rest of the South. Legislation is still being passed to infringe on gay rights, but they ignore their own behavior!

In Arkansas they tried, unsuccessfully, to pass a law stating that people had to use the bathroom intended for the sex they were born with. This was supposed to keep transgender people out of cisgender bathrooms. The idiots behind this nonsense tickled me. How in hell were they going to regulate it—issue permits where you would have to show your pass before you entered, maybe the same passes they had in South Africa for black people? Does that mean all businesses will have to hire a pass checker? Or does that mean they will just have to lower their laundry? And where would they get the money? Like most states, Arkansas is short of cash. But there's enough money for inessentials. What is essential is what feathers their pockets. Transgender people have been around for thousands of years. All of a sudden it becomes a problem that didn't exist before. Why? Fundamentalist preachers have been condemning gay folks for years and years. The bottom line is that fundamentalists and the government should stay out of our bedrooms and bathrooms and clean up their own. What we do is private. Private! Stay out! Maybe if our politicians did the jobs we hired them for, they wouldn't have time to harass any of us.

Most children who are gay are born gay, including in my own family. In my family no one who was gay could speak openly about their sexuality among a bunch of self-righteous Catholic boys, me being one. The boys talked openly about these "queers" and "faggots." No one would dare to come out. Some of my high school classmates would go down to West Hollywood to beat up queers. They thought it was great fun, and we all laughed.

Another close friend revealed—only to me—that he would sleep with a guy if no gal was available. He was a very sensitive guy, and he needed the love. And he was as straight as any married man with five children—kids who really love him.

I've only been propositioned three times in my whole life—once by a woman and twice by men. Both men were close friends who happened to be drunk at the time. It never came up when they were sober, so I never confronted them. I didn't see the point. Both were straight, married men with kids.

This situation is not very clear. Straight or gay is hard to tell. Ignorant, self-righteous religions condemning these men and women is sinful. I think the only sin one can commit is to purposely cause harm to someone else. That's it! It's really that simple. We were created to be joyous, not guilty!

10

CULTURAL VALUES

Confucius Say: Man who masturbates
only screwing himself.

Cultural values are transmitted from one generation to the next, and few really question them. We just go along, blindly following everyone else. I did. Everything seemed normal to me until I reached the age of twenty-seven. I was raised in the fifties and sixties. In elementary school, we boys thought girls were stupid—until the sixth grade when the girls got most of the good grades. At that age we were very impressionable and would swallow all the lies being fed to us without question. The lies came from our churches, our government, our peers, and our educational system. Our teachers painted my Native American brothers and sisters as savages, when we were the ones who savaged the earth and anyone who got in the way. My black brothers and sisters were called slurs and assessed as ignorant and stupid, while the white slaveholders denied them the right to education and then cooked the books to deny them their fair wages for labor. Today we still see the results in poor housing opportunities and low wages. Poverty is always a result.

The same thing happened to other immigrants, even the Irish and Italians who are my ancestors. There used to be signs on businesses stating "No Irish hired here!"

You can't bring the best out of people by treating them as subhuman. But there is some progress here in the South. Here in Arkansas, many of the black massacres are now recorded as white massacres. We are slowly moving in the right direction. All of these historical events influence us, especially in our sexual views of other races. That makes these people subject to illegal, legal laws that forbid interracial marriage. How many black men were hung or shot for looking at a white woman? We are here to love freely, guided by the love in our hearts. All else fails miserably. You can't legislate the heart, and only fools try.

Women make up 50 percent of the world's population and are the ones who still face the most discrimination worldwide. It makes no sense. They raise our children and are our lovers and companions. They hold the feminine mystique, which balances male aggression. If we used that balance, we could end war and environmental destruction. I think our children would like that. Just imagine what that would be like.

Our culture teaches men to be strong physically. We're not taught to be emotionally or spiritually strong. It is our emotional and spiritual strengths that get us through the tough challenges of life, our self-doubt, and confusing times.

We can balance both. Vets do that, when out the love they have for their friends, they very willingly take a bullet for their buddies. Balance is always the key using both our masculine and feminine sides. War is horrible, and we should avoid it. But this is one positive compensation. We could all take advantage of that when they come home.

11

SEXUAL OPTIONS

Confucius say: Man who lay on back, be bed ridden.

Sexual union is one of the best ways to cool off or just blow off steam. It's much better, for example, than beating a pillow to death or slamming your crockery against the wall. Pussy is easy to understand. It's super sweet! But have you ever been treated like a princess or a prince? When you read all those fairy tales in childhood, you may have imagined you were a princess, off in some foreign land being saved by some handsome prince. What if that could happen every weekend in your bedroom? What if you're the princess and your lover is the prince right here, right now—not in France or Italy or China?

What has made us think so little of ourselves? Read Quodoushka, Tantra, and the Kama Sutra. They will open doors you can't even imagine. Your heart is the passkey. Can you imagine yourself as a god or a goddess—a god who rules himself with wisdom and compassion or a goddess who rules herself with love, empathy, and understanding? That's not easy. I recommend starting with the prince and the princess, and the rest will follow. Put yourself in the hands of the Great Spirit, who created you to seek divine sexual union. You will no longer be self-centered, and you will have a permanent relationship based on love and respect.

You will be treated with respect and equality. You will no longer be treated as a mere sex toy. Lust will merge into love and, eventually, divine love, in which you will finally feel truly as one with your partner. That mythical state was mentioned in church, but as usual, no instructions were given on how to get there. It's just as well; the blind leading the blind always fails. Your health will shift in divine union. Casual sex with multiple partners leaves you wide open to getting STDs. Making love makes that visitor unlikely. Divine sexual union makes that impossible. Yeah, right! That's because your vibrational level becomes so high it will burn up any disease organisms. They can't take the heat! Remember, this is union with God (All that was, all that will be and all that is!) Within God, only the positive exists. Now that's a free taxi ride to heaven. Get on board.

Have you ever wondered why churches belittle sex? You can forget about them ever explaining divine sexual union. Why would they tell you that it can take you on a free trip to heaven? Did you ever have such a joyous trip in church? When did you ever have a divine orgasm in church? A high level of loving in the bedroom will translate out into the entire house, where love and respect become normal.

Eventually everyone gets treated as special. That special love will spread out throughout your neighborhood, your city, your state, and our whole country. It can even grow to the point where war stops. Yes, that's possible! Happy people don't kill each other. Compassion and cooperation will abound. You will actually know your neighbor. Can you believe that? Maybe I'm dreamin'.

About twenty years ago I asked my angels how to stop war. You see, I spent two years in the Peace Corps in Liberia (West Africa). Since then, I have been very active in the peace movement. I asked my angels how many of us would have to fast to stop war; they said 50 percent. How many of us would have to ask for angelic help? 60 percent. How many of us would have to make love? 50 percent. I don't know about you, but it was an easy decision for me. There's always an abundance of spiritual help available to us, but it's not a free ride. We have to do our part. If you ask for help to lose weight, you will get it. But you are the one who is the fork operator. The buck stops there.

I am a master organic gardener and can garden successfully in any part of our country. But until I get off my butt and plant the seeds, nothing happens. And unless I do the weeding, thinning, and watering, I won't get much. When we do our share of the work, we will get good results. Nature always helps willingly in all her forms. I talk to too many people who put themselves down, saying they didn't do anything, God did it all. Nonsense, it's a partnership! He is not going to plant the seeds or hide your fork. He's not going to do your massage or your operation. That's why many weak prayers go to hell in a handbasket.

12

BEDROOM ETIQUETTE

Confucius Says: Man who lay woman on
ground have peace on earth. "Amen Brother!"

Always ask your partner what he or she likes. Never assume
anything. You know what they say—assuming something
makes an ass out of you and me. Guilty as charged! What
you wear in the bedroom is up to you, but discuss it. A
woman can turn on a guy too fast. You don't want to miss
the sensual making out or the hot foreplay before he sticks
his hard dick into your hot pussy. Always take the time to
build up your passions. Take all the time you need to fully
please each other! Hell, where are you going anyway? When
you don't have the time for a sexual encounter, Tantra has
a nurturing position that sets you up for later on. Tantra
teaches you to take the time when you make love.

They suggest you set a room aside for a weekend special. You get to be the maître de! Have beautiful flowers and sensual music. You can add incense, photos, or whatever else you'd like. They suggest you take two to three hours to make love. It could begin with a massage—foot or full body. They say to leave the cell phones outside. My attitude is that I came in here to make love to my partner, not Ma Bell or Papa Verizon. Focus on your partner. That lack of focus is one of the main reasons for divorce. When your partner is making love to a cell phone or a TV, you are left out. I think I'm more important than that. And so are you.

Always take the time all the way through if you're a male pleasuring a female partner. Do it until *she* is satisfied—not you. If she goes until she comes that's great. Ask her. No two women are exactly alike, nor are any two men. Ask! I think you cheat your partner when you don't eat her pussy till she comes. No wham bam, thank you, ma'am. Oral sex is extremely pleasurable. It's the only way some women can experience a full orgasm. Just warming up that box doesn't do the trick. She deserves it all, and so do you. A good blow job is never turned down on the front or back end. Sweet stuff! It always feels good to us and her as long as we don't cram our dicks down her throat, drilling for Chinese gold. You could settle for a little US silverware. There's a sweet spot on the roof of a woman's mouth, concave in shape, that is very pleasurable for a blow job, for both the man and woman. She can work your penis into that spot for some super sucking that won't choke her out. Done right, it's awesome and both partners will be fully satisfied. Go for it!

Any good marriage is founded upon mutual respect where both of your needs come first. That requires focus and commitment, along with time to build up. *Wham bam, thank you, ma'am,* does not work. Without mutual respect, there is no real love. The marriage will probably fail, and the kids will be caught in the middle. Abuse is likely to follow. Our children deserve the best long-term support possible. Marriage is no big deal until you raise kids. Then you need to hang in there till the job is done. Although I realize abuse can change all that. Children who watch their parents beat each other up are unlikely to grow into healthy adults, even with therapy.

I have an old friend who was beat with a coat hanger. Today in his seventies he is a recovered alcoholic, but he still finds it very difficult to discuss with even his closest friends. With mutual love and respect, you learn to love each other and become good models for your children. Then they learn how to love each other, which means you take care of each other in the bedroom. Sexual union should be central. I mean hells bells, it is a lot of fun. Always take enough time to make love and always show the mutual love you have for each other to your kids, with lots of hugs and kisses—for the kids too!

Study Tantra, and you will see some amazing lessons. Ever had anyone make love to you for two to three hours? They do! Please take the time for each other. Respect and honor begin in the bedroom. Don't forget how important you are. Love each other well. I would recommend taking one full week to go to a special place to make love—again, no phones. I did that for one week at the Kings River. My partner and I made love in the morning, and during the day we went fishing and canoeing. We both loved the outdoors. I was in hog heaven (without the hogs) and had never felt so energized. Good lovemaking will not wear you out. If it does, then hit the gym—hard.

We went to the mountains because we love them. Go somewhere you love. How about that special place you always wanted to share with the one you love but didn't think you could afford? Dream big! It's just an annual trip. Save up. Can you give up something you really like for the one you love? You know you will never forget those trips. You'll collect a lifetime of memories. You know, we never did it again. We were too busy raising our last kid and too busy doing our own things. That was a big mistake.

13

HEART-TO-HEART

When you make love, always use a heart-to-heart connection. Tantra has a great one.

The simplest way I know to form a heart-to-heart connection is the following example. The couple stands face-to-face. The man places the palm of his hand on the woman's heart while he looks, with deep love, into the woman's eyes and says, "I love you." The woman does the same by placing her palm upon his heart and saying, "I love you," while looking into his eyes. This simple exchange of energy is powerful and will shift your energy out of your root chakra and into your heart chakra. In time you can even go higher. Open them up wide. Don't hold back. This process will improve your sex life beyond what you can imagine now. Don't hold back, and don't have any doubt. After all, you are following your soul's lead. Some of you don't believe me. Your soul is your heart connection. It does not make mistakes. This applies to straight and gay. The soul knows all of you as equals. You can use a heart-to-heart connection with anyone, anytime, anyplace—your mother, father, and so on—even your enemies if you can get close enough!

A heart-to-heart union is especially important with all your children. In a very practical way you can help them accept the sexual bodies they have as being normal. Quoushaka teaches that you have nine different sexual organs, and all are perfectly normal. In the illustrations you will find them. It would be wonderful if mothers sat down with their daughters, using the photos to show that your daughters pudendum is normal. The illustrations show their love lips (labia) are quite normal. You should do this while naked, both of you, so she can see you're normal too. Fathers should do the same if you can with your sons. I can remember in a high school gym class, while undressing how all of us were looking at each other's dicks, hoping we didn't have the smallest one. Nobody said a word. I still chuckle today!

Better to do this with your kids rather than them being unnecessarily embarrassed by the other kids. You can even get your outspoken kids to tell the others where they can find the information. Most kids are sincerely looking for reliable sexual information. They want to know. They are entitled to know. Period.

The toughest part is cleaning out your own heart, your own baggage. Old hurts will trip you up for life. They can confine you too an earthly hell unless you get the help you need. You then become worthless to live with. You're always living in the past and can't address the present in a meaningful way. I know; I lost a very good woman this way. She'd been married four times but could not clean out all her baggage, even with the best intentions. Remember what Yoda said, "Don't try, do!" This includes cleaning up any PTSD that comes from rape or incest. This also includes the PTSD of many of my military buddies. Your life will be worthless if you don't. It is well worth the effort. I was in the 4th Infantry division in Pleiku in 1970. Many of you went through a living hell there. Tap the courage you used there. I know it's tough and much easier to give this advice than follow it. Take one step at a time, and you will get there. As the Chinese say, "Each journey begins with the first step." One step you can take is to join a veteran's outreach group. You can google US Armed to Farm Sustainable Agricultural Training for Military.

NWA Veterans start community gardens to inspire other vets. Also google *Farmer Veteran Coalition, Arkansas*. One of the best things you can do is get away from the cities and get back to nature where there is peace and quiet and time to contemplate. I wish you the best! What the hell, you gave the best!

I have been really tough on the Catholic Church, in which I was raised. Here's why. Besides my early elementary education that was highly distorted (in chapter 1) I went to a Catholic High School that was only for boys. I followed that with four years at a Catholic College that was also boys-only. I was a Goody Two-shoes and went at my parents' request.

But my parents were some of the best, and I haven't met any who are any better. So off to Loyola I went.

I majored in biology and took courses that included anatomy and physiology where there was no mention of sexuality. We were just taught about all the parts, including the pudendum (pussy in street language), labia, vagina and clitoris, uterus, and ovaries. The rest we had to figure out ourselves. That was not a problem for a bunch of boys. We were very willing to experiment outside of the classroom. We also had eight semesters of ethics and philosophy, where again, there was no mention of sex. What the hell would ethics ever be needed for in the bedroom? Amazing! You know, it was just like being in auto shop and being told all the parts that went into an engine after never being given the car manual.

I was at Loyola in the sixties and wondered if anything had changed in thirty years, so I read a Catholic college teaching manual on personal behavior. I borrowed it from a friend who was teaching non-Catholic girls who wanted to become Catholic. *Nada! Nothing!* I was not surprised. I remember how Copernicus and Galileo were treated. Remember, the Earth is square, and so is the Catholic Church! But I do have to thank them for teaching me a strong sense of ethics, even though they still shortchange women.

God bless you all!

FINAL NOTES

Porn: The American Bar Association (ABA) has a website on the effects of pornography on children. They see a lot of this in court and find it very difficult to counter. Some porn is benign, at least somewhat, because only photos are shown. It's the videos that really mislead kids into thinking that's the only way to fuck (always their word of choice). They think they are "porn masters." Are they? A master of anything treats all participants as equals and does not drive the equation. That is done out of love and respect.

There are many books about sex now, which is a great change from back in my day. You can get books for children and teens. Check them out. Those of Christian origin tend to be wishy-washy. You can't blow smoke up kids' butts today. It's foolish to even try! Kids' curiosity is insatiable. They can't get enough information, and that is perfectly normal. When the hormones kick in, everything changes. As a parent I think it is extremely important that they not be left out to dry in ignorance. And what is taught in most schools is worthless. So reboot!

In a previous chapter, I told you about a woman who gave her son a copy of *Playboy* but told him these were idealized women and didn't look like most women. Children must be informed of the truth, or they will end up like I did. When I was about thirteen years old some boys were talking about sex. They said their parents did it. I was shocked and thought, *Not my parents*. But with a little reflection, I realized they'd been telling the truth. I had great parents—some of the very best. I was with them for twenty-one years, and not once did I ever hear them argue. And they raised eleven kids. It can be done. It takes unconditional love and the willingness to always forgive.

Thank God for our voluptuous bodies erected for mutual pleasure! When sex is practiced on a love level, it is the glue that holds families together. It is not the churches and governments who have surreptitiously taken its place. That power lies within us. We were made to be happy, loving children of God. The Creator knew what he/she was doing we were not made to run around in sackcloth and ashes, feeling guilty about our natural, God-given inclinations. Hooray!

AFTERWORD

Writing this book and sharing all this information with you has been a real pleasure for me. This information has changed who I am. I am a much better person than I was ten years ago. It can do the same for you! Using the full power of your human sexuality will do that for you too.

There is too much information in this book for most people to handle well. Use what you can now; the rest will follow in time. This is a long haul but a very pleasant one. Enjoy the ride, and take your angels with you. This book would not have been possible without mine. You can even ask them to help you make your sex life awesome. If you don't know what to say, you could ask them for an MBO, most benevolent outcome. They will do their best to help all the participants to have the most benevolent outcome possible under the current circumstances. Ask them to keep you focused on what you have to do, and ignore the whole world that seems to have gone batshit crazy!

But we're not all nuts. I see a lot of women asserting their positive power to heal. The MeToo movement is one example. Greta Thunberg is another female warrior, who took on the whole UN council at eighteen years old and four foot one, making all of them look like bunch of tools. These movements scare the hell out of the establishment. That is the military-industrial establishment that Eisenhower warned about when he left office. "If you don't get the military industrial complex under control, you will lose your democracy." And that is the way it seems when the world is batshit crazy. But this is the time when humanity has to balance the masculine with the feminine. We are in the birth throes where there's always blood, sweat and tears.

The old order is dying and struggling to survive. And, as pointed out in this book, you have the power in your own bedroom and in your own family to begin shifting us out of war and into peace. When the war between the sexes stops, so will war itself! So go make love, and rejoice in that God-given spiritual power. Don't forget to laugh. Much of life is absurd!

Namaste!

ILLUSTRATIONS

- Quodoushka's Female Anatomy Types
- Primarily based upon the labia.

Sheep woman

Cat W.

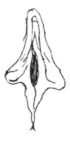

Bear

Buffalo

Wolf

Women

Antelope Woman

Deer W.

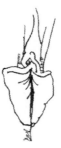

Fox W.

Dancing

Women

Economic   Image   and Takers Religious + cultural
                Makers

                Sculpting   Armoring

                Family and   Relationship

                        Bi Sexual

                Sexual   Preferen

Hetero Sex   omni   sexual   Homo Sex

                Ambi Sexual

TANTRA SEXUAL POSITIONS

Yab yam - favorite

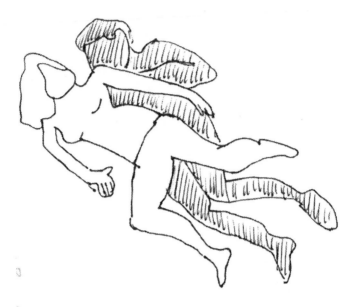

Spoon

TANTRA

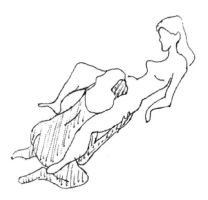

Cunnilingus

Scizzors

MEDITERRANEAN
FOOD PYRAMID

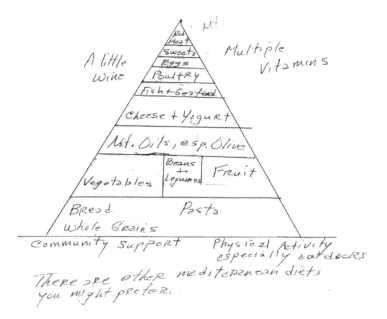

A little
Wine

Mt.
Red
Meat
Sweets
Eggs
Poultry
Fish + Seafood
Cheese + Yogurt
Mst. Oils, esp. Olive
Vegetables | Beans + Legumes | Fruit
Bread   Pasta
Whole Grains

Multiple
Vitamins

Community Support   Physical Activity
                        especially outdoors

There are other mediterranean diets
you might prefer.

SEXUAL OPTIONS!

	Having Sex	Making Love	Divine Sexual Union
1.	Crotch Centered	Heart Centered	Soul Centered
2.	Treated as a pussy	Treated as a princess	Treated as a Goddess
3.	Self centered	Other centered	Soul centered
4.	Temporary	Permanent	Cosmic
5.	Lust	Love	Divine Love
6.	STD's Likely	STD's Unlikely	STD's Impossible
7.	War, Likely	War, Unlikely	War - Impossible!
8.	Environment, ignored	Env. - protected	Env. - Love of ???
9.	Bedroom - Uncertainty	Respect	Honor
10.	Add your own!		
11.			

REFERENCES

1. Ananda - Making Love to God. The Path to Divine Sex.
2. Anastasia - Ringer Cedars of Russia: Book #1
3. Gina Ogden: "Women Who Love Sex and The Heart and Soul of Sex
4. Kama Sutra
5. Kinsey: Dr. Kinsey and The Institute of Sex Research
6. Masters and Johnson Research
7. Mother Mary Anna, Mother of the Magdalenes
8. Quodoushka

All these books are available online.

Park Bench Trilogy/Making Love Forever-MORE

Printed in the United States
by Baker & Taylor Publisher Services